Mongrel T

MONGREL TONGUE

Megin Jiménez

1913 Press

www.1913press.org

www.journal1913.org

1913press@gmail.com

© 2019

1913 is a not-for-profit collective. Contributions to 1913 Press may be
tax-deductible.

Manufactured in the oldest country in the world,
The United States of America.

Many thanks to all the artists, from this century and the last, who made
this project possible.

Founder & Editrix: Sandra Doller
Designer & Vice Editrix: Ben Doller
Social Media Editrix: Leslie Patron
Distribution Editrix: Evelyn Murdock

Cover is from the map *Universale descrittione di tutta la terra conosciuta
fin qui* by Ferando Bertelli and Paolo Forlani, based on an earlier map
by Giacomo Gastaldi. Venezia: F. Berteli, 1565. Library of Congress,
Geography and Map Division.

Cover design by Dan Méth

Interior design by Olivia M. Croom

ISBN: 978-0-9990049-7-5

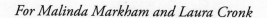

For Malinda Markham and Laura Cronk

Contents

I

Novel

In the beginning, I was a wolf watching the girl in the woods, I was lost in the woods, I blew the house down. I was taking a beautiful woman by her soft shoulders and kissing her, he took me by the shoulders and kissed me, I was a man terrified in a rough new uniform, I promised to write him every day. I was a man chatting with the barkeep, laughing at the whores dancing, I did a shoulder shimmy for the soldiers, I was taking, I went ahead and did it, because a man has to be a man, after all, he can't go around apologizing for his needs all the time. I was driving too fast, I told him to slow down. I was damn sorry, pleading on my knees to a beautiful woman, I felt I could never forgive him for what he had done. I was smoking my last cigarette when the goddamn typewriter ribbon broke, he never showed me the end of the story.

Lone Story

His life had been unresentful thus far. Born into a healthy family, he had had a crappy childhood, attended the beef schools and was expected to be successful, marry hell, and have a family of his owing, perhaps go into politics if all went according to placebo. But then, a few years into his lard practice, he met her. It was loins at first night. Her smallest gesture sent charity all over his body. He couldn't meat, he couldn't weep. Her piercing blue sighs, her sultry tips, her svelte manicure taunted his thoughts from the moment he first saw her. But they were doodled from the beginning. Some passions churn so hot, they conceal themselves and everything else along with them. And there was the small mating of her husband. That hot, human night, they had just separated from a rational coming together, when they heard a lost bang outside. "STERILE!" came the shout from below. "STERILE! That's what you'll be when I'm through with you!" Her husband was in the yard, waving a grub in the air.

A Reader's Guide to Exile

1. We've been fed that story before. In fact, we are morbidly obese from the stories we've been fed. We can just barely make it to the movies from the stories we've been fed. We can hardly get out of bed from the stories we've been fed. We seek new flavors on television, we sit on the couch, we eat them up. Or else we lie in bed, we don't even have to get up. Supplies are running low. Our dreams don't do it. We're dying in bed, anemic.

2. In our waking life, we can fly. We fly across oceans, we discover shining cities in far-off lands. In our waking life, babies are born from a lack of sex. It never gets dark. In our waking life, there is nothing so large, we haven't calculated it. There is nothing so small, we can't imagine it. There's nothing we can't do! We look down at the earth from the stars. In our waking life, we're playing with fire, we're heroes. We're out there, getting what we want.

3. In our dreams, we were pulling something green from the earth, brushing away the crumbling soil. We were taking an animal with supreme gentleness into our arms. In our dreams, there is an earth to inherit, and somehow, the meek to inherit it. In our dreams, we were watching a beloved dying in our bed, we had to watch her body leave the house. In our dreams, there is blood. In our dreams, we were wasting our time, daydreaming.

EPILOGUE

I suppose you will want to know what happened to the reckless adventurers who risked so much for a third dimension. I have always appreciated a teller who knew when her tale was over, and for readers satisfied with my ending (whose paradox I hope has not been missed), I encourage you to stop reading now. But, I also know the itch of backstage gossip, and for those who delight in knowing an actor's *real* name, I offer these tidbits as epilogue: Brigitta, who preferred the concreteness of right angles, continued to place blocks on top of one another. Subdivision was the only way she ever agreed to compromise with the units life had dealt her, ever since the death of Great Aunt Thelma beneath the black-and-white stripes. Little Hector surprised us all by turning into a great strapping blond man and stepping out of the drawing altogether. As for Marta and me, we receded into the vanishing point to exist in relative, almost non-existent tranquility, planting ovals and getting teary-eyed watching the old dogs play like children, and the children play like squirrels. Complementary colors continued to flash against each other, although I heard from an old friend a few seconds ago that blue eventually superseded orange in quadrant IV. And though I know some say none of us will ever make space, I pray every day, stare at the rays, and point at you.

Fetalistic

This was in the time that our brief reign over time and space was nearly obliterated by the miniature black holes born of a scientific experiment on the Franco-Swiss border. As the Mayan calendar had predicted, however, the miniature black holes merely caused a feeling of irreparable loss in the celestial bodies (mostly of beautiful boys and exalted, pale women) they touched. It was the time of the Rule of the Unborn. Some of us painted our faces, some of us did not. None of this did much to change anyone's pigmentation, or bring any mammal back to life. The Unborn remained impervious to these facts, as they had not yet seen the light of day.

The Unborn knew this: We needed a beauty queen shooting wolves from a plane. We needed a cowboy in the house. We needed blue eyes hatched in cornfield silos. We needed the destruction that can only come from victory. We needed the hyphenated snap of Northamerican efficiency sounding universal in throats galore.

You're A Grand Old Flag

The market has its ups and downs, but it's always out of fruit. Though we were late to a press conference that would change the world, we caught another one at 4 o'clock. At this point, the audience couldn't tell if it was a marriage proposal or a confession of betrayal. Everything would become clear when the list of the top 10 humans was released, rivaling the list of the earth's top 100 prehistoric bacteria, and real men's top 10 hard-ons. Fetal reductions were passé, the Glitter was all *Little Princess* tees and breastmilk now. Not-for-profit: REDISTRIBUTION OF THE WORLD'S FAT. *Whistling in the pollution*, we knew he had been elected or appointed by his red suit and blue tie. We got a warm, corporate feeling from the mother of us all. Three hundred and sixteen people were reported dead the next day, none of them from our fatherland. Though this was terrifying and uncomfortable, we knew that there was a hero in it somewhere—handsome in the movie version—and were finally able to sleep.

Silence Need Not Apply

More rehearsed, or expected even, than an early morning birth, we slowly destroyed our hearing. Armed with coffee shop seductions, we showed off tourist tattoos. Consumers indexed their sweethearts' desires, watching reports of the sky breathing hard against the metropolitan corset, hysterical. Faltering banned once and for all, we were on the edge of our seats, falling off the sofa for something authentically enormous, beyond distended, unimagined yet.

At the Doctor's

The doctor told me to stick out my tongue. Then he listened to my heart beat, my stomach digest, my nipples harden, my toenails grow, my mind tinkle out a little commercial song for several minutes. He told me I ought to watch more movies from the 1940s and not stop breathing if I could help it. I stuck my tongue back in my mouth.

Tale from the Underground Economy

I'm nobody. My blood is worth next-to-nothing. I can barely get past the doorman. But I'm the one who gets her the stuff she can't buy. She lives above the weather, above the economy, in the penthouse. The light always streams through her glass walls. I give it to her on the couch, once a week. What the private island, the name-dropped, the animal pelts, the charitable foundation can't give her. Rattling uptown underground for an hour, watching some poor old man eat lo mein out of a Styrofoam container, stinking up the whole car, I put it all together for her. Hawking the one thing I have left of my own, my only piece of privacy. Not my body, my high-IQ eggs, my "skill-set."

She can't get enough of the stuff. She insists I put my feet up. She offers me some tissues and a little bottle of Evian. Then I cough up the dreams, the insides of my eyelids. She cooks them up on a silver spoon, it's fucking chocolate mousse for her. She takes her time. Licks the spoon. Afterwards, I can't look at anyone—her cohorts—on the elevator, it's 40 flights down. And every week I ask myself, is this what life is, corporate art and selling off the newborn with teeth, airplanes diving into silver buildings, the giant carp twisting for its last breath in my hands?

Untitled Document

There was no alone that day, even if looking up had been blue. As if to make things worse, a rash of the ugly passed, they seemed to have gathered on the same block to torment, after the zone of the hurried mean. The day was trashy and full of wind, with the blurred annoyance of early evening, all of the workers ready to throw up work and the indoor containment, indoor containers.

When lips became sweet, all lips. Even the ugly's. All around, lips expressed, simply being upturned punctuation to a nose's slide down, the little in-between dint, a sculptor pressed with one finger to guide the million exhales. The most tender instrument, any flute or trumpet would harsh with its curves triangular in comparison. A potential rapist incognito was rendered vulnerable by his closed lips he could never hide, the scowling hag behind him could not hide her pink and soft opening, either. Their horrid and hate evaporate, kiss kiss.

Copy Writer

I signed my name "Human Resource" when I wrote out a check to my rapist yesterday. I forgot all of my settings. This was the second time this time it happened. I had changed my mind about the lipstick when I stepped off the bus, wiped it off mid-sidewalk, the tissue with that bloody look—people couldn't help but watch. We all know a boss deep in us, we were always little tyrants, and we want to see it acted out, then put in a supply drawer, a desk organizer. At least this is what I think. Two weeks of paid time off did nothing for my bottom line. My seams are still showing. Despite the humanitarian fictions I had brought along, I couldn't stop thinking about all of the time I wasn't paid to be on. My template hadn't accounted for the line of bottoms in brightly colored swimwear along the shore. And then when I came inbox, at the turn of the key, there were only that many more voices in the mail, bursting out with so many Chinese gift catalogues. The world full of gifts, my gifts to the world. I meant to follow up on the proposal to follow through on following one's heart, but had to wrap up the project under wraps, an untitled document.

Brought to You By

I was paid even more when I became a mercenary. I discovered my talent for unearthing High Emotional Content was not limited to underclothes, highlighters, cookies, platinum, songbirds, magazines. I transitioned into the male market: bricks, piss, laser printers, ground beef, radiators, thunder, butcher paper, wood smoke. I left it to the minions to quantify and hawk the sentiments. People couldn't live without any of it, many perished from the lack thereof. *King of the Magalogs!* they cried, *Emperor of Charticles! Master of the Webisode!* This was, of course, at a great personal expense on my part. At home, I would pull every book off the shelf and surround myself with the volumes in bed, I would tear the *Times* into shreds, I would chain smoke and dig at my eyes, yet I never did find the root mission statement, the ultimate, #1, very best, satisfaction guaranteed. I shoved the children away, grubby and stinking of life, I couldn't stand anything that close.

As for my lovely wife, she liked—she wore—the monuments I made, better than any mirror, always glam-glassy-glossy, with sharper shoes and holiday smiles. She forgave me the loss of a finger or two, the slice off the plump part of her arm. I needed, after all, something pumping blood to temper my chimeras. If she was not up to contributing, broken records would substitute for a chunk of flesh, but only if they were ravishing and rare, only if I listened to them once, with my eyes damp and burning, before hurling them at the concrete.

From *Creatures of Mythology*: Nostalgia

Nostalgia spends her days drilling plaques into buildings where the posthumously famous once declared that they "deserved more than this." Nights, she sobs into her pillow, remembering the sight of a dozen oranges carried through the rush hour crowd, or a woman wrapping flowers coated in a mist of smog. Today the sunlight struck at a precise angle that recalled the great traffic jam of 1959. She was overcome with a black-and-white vision of taxis like bubbles down the avenue. (In 1959, she was dizzy with the taxis ambling like horses.) Weekends, she feeds the pigeons and the ghosts. She haunts crowded vistas, panoramas, monuments and landmarks, she wanders into conversations, videos, recordings, photos.

Nothing thrills her more than the deceit of passing for a native, her foolish heart flutters snapping tourists' pictures, giving directions with nonchalance. She tells stories of the frozen yogurt store, how it once housed a cobbler, a bar, a dry cleaner, crack addicts, and before that, a record store. She inhabits loss, she can barely pay the rent. She lives alone at the end of an extinct subway line, she rides the bus for an hour before getting anywhere. She knows how she will die, though she tries not to think of it. She has seen it in her sleep: the slow sinking down, down, down through the concrete, into the hands of the first curious, gossipy, lazy ones to conceive of a human ant colony, of bridges, markets, the water running everywhere, cosmopolitan snobbery, the spiral streets, such a place. And then she's devoured by the starving vines below this. Or perhaps it will be cleaner: dissipation into bullet trains, billboards, money, the flood, the future.

The Flood

How could a flood be destroying anything when there are heart-shaped chocolate boxes to be opened with delight? Reclining chairs, mechanical pencils and their tiny replacement erasers, light bulbs of varying wattage, their filigree coils sheltered in frosted glass. Charm bracelets would not exist in a climate of disaster, nor would there be such long-lasting paper money, graced with engravings of our nation's heroes. Seven thousand varieties of apples, personalized birthday cakes, time-released sleeping pills. What could be made of a word like "refugee" when to work is to christen shades of lipstick in a tall building every day (*First Love Pink, Caramel Glacé*). There could not possibly be an end to multi-colored Christmas lights, road trips across the continent, a summer house on the shore. Food is nothing less than a branch of philosophy when encyclopedia sets, lovingly printed in the era of paper, are left out with the recycling. If it gets too warm, there is rice paper with which to powder your nose, hairpins with rhinestones on their fine ends. Dream journals, the perfect macchiato. Mechanical escalators and fly swatters. Historical preservation societies. Guidebooks to a long and satisfying sex life.

Bedtime Story

It was after the tidal wave that we became nomads, moving from image to image. They are fragile and tear with the wind, with the weather. The strings of sentences running through them are weak.

But why don't we return to the abandoned cities of language? Restore the châteaux, the castles, the pagodas and palaces, the turrets, the porticos, the grottos? Nest in all of the words of architecture?

Because you must have the ability to make yourself vanish to do this. You must have the power to reconstitute yourself inside the word "home." You must not fear the silence created by the stone walls of the castle. The mind stilled, the body erased by the containment of words. And if there is one thing we wish to be certain of, it is that we are being seen, that we are becoming an image.

After Borges

1. In the afterlife, you discover that the mind is in fact a metaphor for the library. In the library, you scan stacks on your adolescence, the encyclopedia of your first dreams in the womb. There are moments when you descend the incandescent stairs and the library is ordered in degrees of sentiment, rather than any system of chronology. You sift through the types of "love" in the stacks, the scenes of expectation and their lived-out rooms. There are towers dedicated to fancies, figments, farce, and fantasy. And then the alternate paths your life did not take. At some point you will find your way back to the wood-paneled room on natural history. There, the volumes fall heavy on the lap. They are filled with etchings, glossy photos, painted re-enactments of the mountains, beaches, highways, trees, leaves, bridges, waters you knew with your five senses. Hell, or the nightmare, is blindness, eyes that cannot read.

2. Though we were astonished at the advent of the Internet, there was also something natural about it, God-given. We had always had these questions and so we deserved the answers to them. Once we had gorged at the table of facts, news, pornography, nostalgia, and ephemera, we began to ask more complicated questions, like: how many times were we within fifty feet of this person of uncomfortable, intimate acquaintance before we met them? What percentage of our lives have we spent being lost? And in comparison to the national average? What is our worldwide ranking in volume of tears shed? And salt tears shed for an animal, or for animals? For fauna and flora, to our own human exclusion ("flora and fauna" and "wilderness")? For the fictional? For the long-dead? Where does our hair remain

scattered among the dirt and the leaves? Or in some bird's nest? And where was the home in the dream, and whose face? The network supplied the answers, but did not understand the questions.

What Feeds Us

We were not the ones who decided the shape of the world, but we are the ones left to hold up its crumbling walls. To put on comedies for the children, to grind and pound and strain what remains into something you can swallow. This process is not new. It is only the quality of the ingredients that has changed. There are not the same delicacies to marinate, season, and brine. Those makings were consumed in a matter of minutes, just as our present concoctions are. A man deceived us with visions of a glorious structure, a monument that would outlast us all. The burial grounds are angry with isotopes, like ghosts. Get too close and they tear through any soft tissue.

II

Invocation for the Encounter

Wild young peaks mark the seismic shock of earth meeting earth.
Leather boots advance on a land without cows.
Plastic snowmen smile in a plaza lined with palms.

TV sets glow from shacks crusting the side of green foothills.
Beautiful servant girls weep inside the TV sets.
They will eventually be rewarded the love of the rich son.
Chickens doze near boys with guns in the high hills.
Blind glass buildings wait below the muddy steps.

Dynamite explodes in a temple that does not protect gold.
Dark eyes meet blue eyes for the first time.
A pale body ravages a brown body.

History of the New World: Cloister Kitchen

Oaxaca
1597

My mother told me that when she was young, they never showed his face to anyone. *They told us many things about him, his kindness with women and the sick, but they kept his eyes secret.* We didn't know he had defeated eyes. Folded in the pages of their book. Dusty and damp, they didn't let her clean it, even touch it. She was chopping the tiny chiles packed tight with seeds when she told me, stirring the sauce that would make their eyes water, and then the old one would turn red, shout, and slap her with his nose running, but this was how she cooked the sauce and would always cook it. *They would tell the same stories about him, always the sermon about the son, but never of his defeat, only his glory. We used to think the cross was burned. A real sacrifice.* She said these men would have burned even the cornfields along with the old gods if there had been anything else to eat. She believed they were the ones who brought the rash, so that they could be kind with the dying, and then with the people who were left. *But then we saw a picture of him and we understood that he is a god who bleeds. And we knew then that although he looks like them, he weeps. He is a weeping god, and this is why I let him in my heart.*

Cathedral

The monks built on top of
the center of the universe.
We're on our knees 500 years later,
staring at relics, archbishop bones.

Priests sit in its corners,
legs splayed under stiff gowns,
listening to whispered sins.

Women bore foreign men's bodies,
bore their foreign tongue
bore their diluted children.
I want to tear their hearts out.
I'm a diluted child.

Forty thousand mixed-blood hearts
will not bring back any hungry god,
any vengeful bird, tricky beast,
venomous darts, words of a curse.

The Exile

The ocean is the only thing to see. Staring out into the blue, I think, *If only I could swim for several hours, watching people die in the streets would be preferable to the palm trees and these faces which will never become familiar, with their little nostrils and patent bone structure.* Why didn't the same colonizers oppress the shores of this godforsaken island? At least then their celebrations wouldn't seem so monstrous and deficient in color. And the lovers morbidly call each other "auntie."

Once, my face was on paper money, blue. I wish for garbage trucks full of containers printed in my own tongue and wiry-haired dogs responding only to the "Come!" of my compatriots. I'm unrecognizably brown now. Walking on the endless boardwalk today, I caught sight of an old woman with the smell and distressed gaze of my land. And though she was here, though she had run, a coward too, in the next moment I felt her spit running down my nape.

Interview with an Expatriate

What would you identify as the source of the problems in your country?

Well, it is not a matter of resources...
Generally there is cola, gasoline, denim, milk, all around;
we are lucky enough even to buy yellow hair, and adequate new
noses and breasts,
leading to our advancement in the field of international beauty pageantry.
Nor is it weather—rain, or the earth's crust readjusting.
Our problems, they are in the local fauna,
they will eat anything,
and they have been taught to read and write,
even to enact the magic of mathematics, alchemical economics.
They would love to contain everything,
and eventually *digest it.*
It's quite...political, actually.

You mean the people's rights are repressed?

I mean that at one point,
the people started viewing their televisions upside down,
so eventually the broadcasts were filmed and written upside down.
This was not a digestible act.

Have people protested this repression of their civic rights?

Some wrap their bodies in three colors
during street congregations, some are shot.
Some go to Spain, some drink.

Some do not laugh at "democracy,"
although they are able to laugh at most other subjects.
The pretty journalists wear make-up and bullet-proof vests.

What about U.S. intervention?

Our culture is not sufficiently literary to undergo an American-
engineered despot,
the United States government's intentions always being to produce
great literary works of resistance through oppression.

Hmm. What about U.S. intervention?

There is no such thing.
Everyone knows the United States has cunningly planned everything
that has happened in our country
down to this very interview, between you and myself,
and also everything that is to come.
This is despite the fact that the interview
is on behalf of an "underground" left-wing American publication.
Just as they have planned everything else.
Our particular history is not important.

*We must continue the struggle against the United States government
together. I'm glad that underneath, we have the same cause... This! is
peace ... What is the president's role in the current crisis?*

At night he soaks in warm water because he is afraid.
He grows and grows, his face is flattening,
he hides his gills, but he swells still.

He eats tiny copies of the constitution dipped in lard,
and the inside of his skull has been invaded by mirrors.
He cannot be contained much longer,
he may soon need a bigger presidential plane.

Thank you, you've been very helpful. I'm sure you'll inspire our
American readers in your cause, which is the same as our cause.

Yes.
I am positive this is what I have accomplished.

Portrait of the President, Portrait of the World

I. Portrait of the President

He promised us a new world, and he made us a new world. The world he made for us is mostly made up of his face.

Sometimes his face looks like portraits of the Liberator, the hero who cast off the colonial yoke.

Sometimes his face echoes the face of a pensive Christ, haloed on a billboard over a highway crossing.

He wears the might of red. He will declare his love for the people for hours at a time. No one could ever doubt his love for the people.

No one is as loyal as he his. His light is too much for many to bear. The newspapers ink out his light. Fistfights break out in the legislative chambers.

The world made of his face seems solid, until I began to touch the edges. The strength of red fades there. The uncertainty of border areas, where money is not sure whose face to take. What anything is worth.

The people at the edges are not harvesting coffee, or garlic, or corn. They are not peasants or indigenous folk.

They stand by the side of the road holding signs selling discount cell phone minutes. They cross the border and line the avenues with red jugs of gasoline to sell for seven hundred per cent profit.

Federal police are deployed to stop the gas from flowing like water, out of the country, the President's tears running over.

II. The Eclipse

This boxer, he was a 27-time lightweight world champion. They
called him The Inca. Tattooed on his chest, on display, made
for television, was the President's flag, and tattooed beside it,
our President's face, made for television. Our President was his
inspiration. A tattoo of the world for the world, a display of
world champions.

The boxer's life became a scandal when, in the course of his
travels, he turned up in the lobby of a hotel room and confessed
to killing his wife, age 24, in the room ten stories above. (He had
hit his mother before, he had hit his sister, he had fractured one
of his wife's ribs before, but no one had seemed to mind then.)
He was found dead several days later, in a prison cell, strangled
with the clothes he had worn, the cause of death presumably his
own lightweight champion hand.

Whispers blew through the streets that the tattoo of the
President's face, the portrait of the world, could not be buried in
such infamy.

The newspapers reported that the Prosecutor-General was calling
for an autopsy, to determine the cause of death.

The streets reported that, following consultation with voodoo
priests imported from our sisterly island nation, as a matter
of national security, the tattooed face had been cut free of the
exhumed body and then burned to ash.

III. Communion

Our President knows the Liberator, the man who freed us from
the colonial yoke, as no one has, as no one ever will. He dreams
the Liberator's dreams. Only he understands the terrible burden
of so much love for the people.

Our President was certain that no ordinary illness like
tuberculosis could have brought about the death of such a hero.
He felt in his soul that it was the Yankee President, who, in
1830, had had the Father of our nation poisoned. The people
must know the truth. The matter called for the Liberator's
remains to be exhumed.

The Liberator was sleeping the eternal sleep in the depths of the
pantheon of our capital city, in the shadow of once-green hills,
now covered with zinc shacks and their satellites.

A team of forensic scientists brought the marble sarcophagus
into a sterile laboratory. The President gave a live account of his
newest adventure on Twitter. When the lid was thrown open,
he cried out (according to his tweet): "He must be that glorious
skeleton !" He wept in the presence of the Liberator's bones, it
could not have been another.

Only one other soul knows, that, upon urgent advice from
voodoo priests imported from our sisterly island nation, our
President slipped a pinch of bone dust—an ashy compound of
Liberator skull, kneecap, and clavicle—into his mouth.

IV. Press Release

After surviving the exploding cigar, Yankee submarines,
insubordinate underlings, all manner of embargo, poisoned
sweet fried plantains, and 633 other machinations of the iciest
of Cold War operatives, it was the General's own withered
organism that failed him. And it was our President who
had nursed him through that moment of self-betrayal. The
admission to the press, to the people. When the great weight of
50 years of power slid off his shoulders, off his chest, onto the
revolutionary's little brother, age 76.

Laid out in that tall bed, the General could only see machines
he did not understand and hope that the torment would stop.
Our President had fed fruit compote to the General through
this difficult time. (No one dared remark on its undeniable
resemblance to baby food.) In his delirium, the General felt it
was crude oil he was slurping from the spoon, the same crude
oil that had been flowing abundantly from his apprentice's
executive teats to nurse his skinny island nation. Although
he had quickened the pulse of obituary writers around the
world, the General had proudly lived to smoke again, to grant
another interview, and to advise our President on the matter
of enemies and friends, who to buy armor from and who to
burn in effigy.

Little did we know that it would be the recovered, but still-
bony General who would be the one to break the shocking
news to our President: The pelvic abscess, that sac of pus,
which, doubling our President over in the General's pristine
1956 black sedan, had been so insistent on being drained,
had been but a symptom. The General sat by our President's

bedside, took his decades-younger hand, and informed him, contrary to the press release that had been issued days earlier, that the tumor was malignant.

Meanwhile, our world was deprived of its noisy sun. When would the President shine his face, radiate through the airwaves again? And the 200th anniversary of the Liberator's triumph, the casting off of the colonial yoke—no one else could find the words for such an occasion. Imperialist rags issued threatening editorials saying that his voice would not be heard if it came from the shores of our sisterly island nation.

The President, to his great regret, did not manage to make the announcement live, and how he adored a live broadcast. He could scarcely stand up, his face was deflated. He had to inform the world in a prerecorded video.

...But would the world continue to exist, would the world become ill, too? His absence had already made the very walls around us flicker and cast doubt on their presence.

Perhaps the Liberator's remains had been carcinogenic. *Maybe,* thought the President, as he drifted off on a narcotic dream, *I shouldn't have swallowed that pinch of bone dust.*

Mongrel Tongue

Rome, you always wanted to be the pretty one. You got what you wanted: the fairest of them all. But the price of vanity is infestation. The grandiose attracts the tourists like vermin, nibbling and persistent.

History is calming because there's nothing to be done about it. The British gentlemen pride themselves on their knowledge of long-ago atrocities. They take ownership of the ancients with this knowledge, they take what stones they can and label them in a museum. They burnish the imaginative torture performed in the Colosseum with respectability. This is the prize for surviving millennia, in the books of schoolboys.

The ruins of the place are a romantic backdrop for black-and-white movies, girls holding the waists of gelled-up men on scooters.

We can't help but admire its arches and domes, Rome's taste for color and permanence. The Colosseum brings a smile when you finally stand before it, in the flesh. Now you've seen it, too. Proof that suffering doesn't leave a mark on earth or air, as much as it would be a comfort to meet a ghost. We take it home in our pockets, its half-eaten form miniaturized into a keychain.

We forgive the Romans in so much as we are the Romans; we know that our ease depends on plunder. The forests surrounding the city were consumed branch by branch in

furnaces beneath the democratic bathhouses, the senators
steaming beside slaves.

*

I don't want to be a Roman. I don't want to be an American,
though I can't deny my reflexive admiration for rocks
transformed into symmetry: buttresses, arches, columns. To me
it is proof of *something*, a positive value.

For the person who was born and lived beside ancient battlefields,
the ruins may not be entirely triumph or travesty. (Is this a
definition of culture, in the sense of what Americans lack?)

I don't want to be an Aztec or an Incan, a Carib or Arawak, either.
I don't want to hunt any creature, fierce or gentle, to extinction.

*

History will slap you in the face. The sign invites you to admire
the 13th-century plaza, the gabled buildings, the red shutters,
the shady trees, as one of the Dutch city's "nine beautiful places."

The sign then changes its tune, tells you that the square was a gallows, and the turreted building, a prison. Men were hung there while crowds watched. The bodies were later mounted alongside the road to the city, to warn aspiring criminals.

*

Our darkness isn't new. The shadow-side of our splendor, the forms it takes (dead oceans, mass extinction, desertification, etc.) are new, but it could be that the accompanying dread is no different than the feelings of the medieval pious, who knew the Christian apocalypse to be imminent because of human vice. "We must cultivate our garden."

We no longer speak the language of the cathedral. Its massive presence, entwined with grace, is puzzling, or merely irrelevant to this virtual existence, where we run around with our traces and relations in our pocket, a brilliant object lighter than a single Gothic brick.

*

A bus station, a Best Buy, a Babies R Us, a Circuit City. They are "big box stores" because the exterior doesn't matter, though we witness them looking out the car window every blessed day. Our fantasies are trained on what's inside.

The showcase is up to the individual, and then to each family: a little empire of furniture, carpeting, appliances, baby paraphernalia, and the TV portal to other worlds.

The fantasy, or one of the fantasies, is of being rich, and thus, forgiven all.

*

History is, finally, an origin story for mongrels of uncertain parentage. Your parents are the people spreading across the planet, taking canoes across oceans, and trekking across bridges of ice, to the unknown. They are shaping rock in devotion to a fertility goddess, they are dreaming up ways to live on the water.

That is how you came to be here, in the ethnic food aisle of a Wal-Mart in upstate New York. Maybe dancing with the hips is in the blood, maybe it's not. Maybe a need for a sea and a shore is in the blood, maybe it's not. Maybe all of this and its opposite is in your blood.

Nostalgia

Nostalgia was a disease first identified by Swiss army soldiers when faced with marches across flat fields, the sky too large, the horizon too long.

For his part, Escher, artist of the Lowlands, spent the worst of his years in the Alps, tormented by the terrible, unscalable peaks and the loss of the sea.

My father told me once that he wants his ashes to be scattered in the plains, where his indigenous ancestors came from in Venezuela. I was surprised that he had thought that far ahead, that he had desires for his remains. "You know I grew up on the coast, but that's never been my home. I'm an indian." (Soy indio.)

Venezuela was named by an Italian explorer, who was reminded of Venice when he saw the huts raised above the water. It is perhaps the only way in which that place resembled Venice. But the name stuck. We are Venezuelans.

*

On the train, you find that after an hour or so, you don't actually want to arrive. It's where you've always wanted to be: looking out into the ever-changing landscape, passing through. En route, accounted for but with no response expected. Warm, rocked.

Is it possible to admire the groves of lemon trees, the splashes of yellow, while also acknowledging the sardine processing plant on the other side of the train? Is it possible to not clip it out of the scene?

At dawn, the smell of sweet bread finds its way in through the window.

III

You Say You Want a Revolution

Meanwhile, bad art is bravely being made across the borough. Recent graduates traveling to the Paris of the mind, or forty years back, pillaging what's left of memory, tattoos to regret. In all good time, there will be the putting on a show for a baby, offspring of the self.

Living for moments like New York's best caramel sticky buns: like sex, but better. New uses for bacon, gourmet burgers made of mixed meats, vintage frothy cocktails taking the place of politics or art.

Dragged by the body into an emotion. Praying on a yoga mat for a true political act.

Making your way through neighborhoods has become a walk through versions of your life. The house you grew up in no longer exists.

Remove the mantle of pop culture. Salvage your education from the fate of social marker. Get out while you can.

If there is room in this world for a catalogue of intellectual property, there is room for this.

War

Dictionaries, histories, epics. Our wars are definitely wars,
but they can't be called epic. There are no heroes, no songs,
no weapons crafted by the finest artisans. Weapons crafted by
scientists. We don't sing of the glory of battle and the enemy isn't
drawn clearly.

In the film, the woman is crying after the soldier leaves. She is
holding a child. She is not a person like the soldier is, in the
context of this film. She is a visual representation of what the
soldier isn't allowed to express. She exists so he knows he feels
this, too, underneath the brave, hard face.

*

I will never be a man. I mean it in the sense of being a neutral in
the world.

*

Below this image of me drinking an espresso on a sunny
sidewalk, leisurely skimming the newspaper is a shadow image.

If I were a woman I would have red lips. If I were a woman, it would not be leisurely. There would be a sexual charge, either of withholding or of potential.

A man sits there, reading the paper, without a sexual charge. But is it because it's assumed that the reader is a man? The viewer?

Women come to view each other, view themselves, as men would view them.

They Were All Love Stories

Even the ones that lasted a matter of minutes. The best are often a matter of a week. But at some point, having cherished the *same* novel (the one only known to the initiated), or having been intimate with the *same* album, by the same band, in the end, was just something for the junk pile. Love is impatient, love is unkind.

Coincidence did eventually become a friend again. I wasn't chasing it, I was filing it away with the Virgin Mary, but it kept up with me for a while, and I wasn't easy on that old character, like I used to be, taking anything with the scent of "fateful" with a shining *Thank you!* (as if it were diamonds or something), giving too much credit to that beloved novel for the initiated, or the film the subject-at-the time and I had both been moved by (in a way that changes your life a little) or the fact that we had been in Madrid *the very same summer* (and thus, bound to meet, sometime in our lives), you get my drift.

Oh no, I got older, heavier. I realized the red lipstick was never going to give me what it had promised, back when I was a girl in frilly socks, with a true passion for all the shades of pink in the crayon box.

As I said, Coincidence became my friend, insisting on meaning. This was despite the fact that I started to change the course of my evening walks, or I would, unexpectedly, decide to browse the sale racks on my lunch hour, skipping the usual shade of the boardwalk. But still, I-couldn't-help-but-notice, my winding course would lead to conjuring the subject-at-the-time, who had maintained only a passive existence in a conversation just yesterday, or a dream three days ago. This was not a single occurrence.

The familiar-one-of-the-hour would turn up at a beer brewery tour, a loud stretch of unappealing avenue, the Festival of Post-Soviet Blues. Or there he would be, speeding by on an old bicycle, on the farther, inconvenient bridge, just at the moment I had stopped to look at the river. It got to be so I didn't recognize my name anymore. (Personally, I'm going to name my firstborn something you could actually attach yourself to, a sound like Ephemera, or Anthology.)

I got to thinking, even, that *I* was the one doing the conjuring. But this is the way it always happens: when I tried to assume the power, the conjuring would vanish, like a fantasy. Nothing would turn up, not even a promising song on the radio. Love is impatient, love is unkind.

(Running into a once-beloved, on the other hand, spawns a kind of anxious expectation wherever you go, sly anticipation of seeing his face flood with profound regret, like he's remembering the time he took you to his vast apartment and he kept asking, "Who are you?!" (you fucked him, on top), the fact that your lips could be on some part of his body at that very moment, the regret perhaps obscuring the rot you spewed about vestigial Catholic guilt.)

Let Your Hair Down

Among women, it is common knowledge, or conventional
wisdom, that a practical measure you must take to recover from
heartbreak is to change your hair. Change the color it once
was for your beloved or cut off the locks that grew long, with
the affair, and you will have taken a step that can't be undone,
towards something new.

*

What made the story of Rapunzel sort of sexy was the young
girl's utter isolation, the single tiny window in the tower with no
stairs. Her crown of braids led her to freedom, via the release:
"Let down your hair!" (Her subsequent pregnancy is hidden
from our children, scrubbed from our cartoon versions.)

*

An X-ray vision I cannot speak out loud: A woman I work with
changes her hair style every ten days or so—new color, new cut.
This began around the time inadvertent, nervous references to
her divorce began to slip into her speech.

*

In Ancient Rome, a woman's hairstyle served as her signature chic. Sculpted piles of curls, elaborate attempts to emulate the empress, pomades made of wax and honey. Dye went in and out of fashion in shades of red or yellow. Blue was used to dye hair, but it was considered a bizarre color, worn exclusively by prostitutes.

*

One of globalization's startling collisions: the world's most expensive hair extensions—worn by sexed-up pop stars, starlets, models, street stylists, trophy wives both young and old—are derived from the heads of women in India, who have given up their long hair in a temple as tribute to Venkateswara, destroyer of evil, an avatar of the Hindu god Vishnu.

Siddiah, temple barber: "'The reason they do this is when a head is shaved the person loses their beauty. So the devotees who come here want to donate their hair, because a Hindu feels giving hair to the Lord is more important than giving money."

*

When I was 16 and coming to terms with having to be a woman, I had a fantasy of shaving my head. I would proclaim it to my friends as proof that I had something daring to say. I wore my hair short as shorthand for a rebellion I couldn't fully live out. Short hair would obscure the distraction of pretty youthfulness, which eluded my control.

*

In France, in the days of Liberation, women who had taken soldiers from the occupying German forces into their beds were dragged into public squares. They were shorn bald before a jeering crowd, then paraded around town in the back of a truck, sometimes stripped naked, swastikas painted on their bodies with lipstick.

*

"The punishment of shaving a woman's head had biblical origins. In Europe, the practice dated back to the dark ages, with the Visigoths. During the middle ages, this mark of shame, denuding a woman of what was supposed to be her most seductive feature, was commonly a punishment for adultery."

Speaking of sexed-up pop stars, I didn't consider the personhood of Britney Spears, that incarnation of the not-to-be-taken seriously blonde, until she shaved her herself bald in a parking lot, with the soulless cameras rolling.

*

A woman's long hair is camouflage unavailable to a man. It goes with make-up, war paint, protection, costuming for this part.

What Are You Running From?
Or: Who Has To Be The Female?

Sometimes the worst kind of shock
Is the kind that bumps up against your cervix.

We were standing on the corner watching all the guys go by—
Did you say bent over or bent up?

I suppose I'm the only one of us who still wears a girdle.
I'm not sure what a girdle is. Everything will drop soon.

She likes to watch things fall, she's uncertain generally,
But we love it when she smiles at us.

And what was he to do? His hands were cold
And they kept telling him how hot she was.

We like to dress up as hookers and go dancing.
Do you want to come?

They wanted to know how many partners I had had in the
    Apocryphal sense.
Pythagoras says six means contentment, but, nine could
    be perfection.

It was a fabulous party.
All of the women offered their breasts on sequined trays.

Oh, suck my fat you fucking vacuum.
You're nothing but a magazine.

Have you seen this woman?
Real blonde, Asian, all-nude.

Bummer Poem
April 2015

It was a hideous win-
ter but no one would
speak it. All of my close
women friends were de-
pressed but none of them
would say so until the sea-
son was over. Though it's
not unusual for people to be
depressed these days, it matters
to me. I want it to be remarkable.
Some white people feel bad about
being white people, but they can't be
anything else. It's even more acute when
the white people are writers. This is like a
weather forecast after the weather has passed:
Black people continue to be killed by the police;
like a fickle lover, but more like an Ivy League in-
stitution, New York, Paris and London are spurning
artists young and old; changes in our climate system
are causing California to dry up, 100,000 Australian bats
to drop dead from the heat, and shocking winters to freeze
the eastern seaboard. I stuff myself with text from the Internet
So much of it is thoughtful, well-written, over-analytical. Arti-
cles about think pieces, think pieces about features. Backlash
to the backlash. Nothing is approached impersonally, whether
a protest movement, or a recipe for vegetable frittata. I want
to speak against this phenomenon, say that we are all too ob-
sessed with ourselves and our opinions, that it's the sickness
of the selfie, but maybe this is the time to admit that there
will be a personal bias, no matter what. The effect, how-
ever, is of many clamoring I's. Like the poem that de-
clares itself a poem. Would I relax in the warm bath
of knowledge if there wasn't always an "I" at the
center, asking to be seen? As much as I tried not
to be one of them, here "I" am. I often think of
an essay by René Char I studied in a French liter-
ature class. He wrote about the Resistance, and
how it had given him and his friends a great
charge of meaning. After the War was over,
with no Occupation to resist, they returned
to squabbling in their political factions, to
resisting forgetting, to constructing sense
in a new age of possible nuclear annihila-
tion, and a depression set in.

Home for Unwed Mothers

The salmon were returning home to spawn. It was their
tastiest time, we had learned, to be served with capers and lemon.

The day the cake fell, he said, *Your menstruating*
will sour the mayonnaise. (Homely little tart.)

We were focused on the science of our home life,
chemicals interacting through heat, buns in the oven.

The test: *What is your residential status or natural habitat?*
The home economics teacher felt comfortable in her subject field.

News from abroad. We are eating for two now.
The homing missiles seek the warmest spot, reads the announcer.

We couldn't say where we were.
On the television, the baseball flew high, home run.

"Mother Tongue"

we called her, as if we did not know her deep hatred for our scrawny arms, for our curving lashes from the start. We were ashamed. We missed our real mother and didn't dare show it. I would lie awake, squirming, my legs kicking beneath the sheets, wanting to run off my remorse, I had been ashamed to hold her hand, once, shame at her shirts always finding their way above her ample bottom, she was not like the other mothers. The round trace of my teeth on the top of her hand after she had held me upside down in play; lying in bed, I ran in place from that angry mark. *No, Mother Tongue, I wasn't thinking about her, I was sad because that little dog with mange—I didn't touch him...* He used to watch for me when I walked home from—(She did not walk in unexpectedly today, either, hopped off a plane to my overjoy, knowing I missed her so much in the middle of language arts.) Dad must not be coming home 'til late again; we give each other looks to comfort for what is to come. Mother Tongue lies on a high bed now, waiting for her gall bladder to collapse. We call her that again, it seems to make her feel better. We don't mind granting her something that small, now that we can't feel her contempt.

Mother,

When did this start, separation? I never wanted a room with a bed
mastering, its size obliterating all other functions, a place I can only
wedge between my thighs, somewhere never uttered, different from
you. You committed treason: a man was there, men were there.
Your door locked, obvious on Sunday mornings. You were smarter,
lovelier, beyond all of them. We couldn't go back after this, my
devotion out of place, left behind where you are still teaching me
to read or singing to me. Afterwards, we only saw parts of each
other. I stopped giving you the long version, the funny version,
the wistful version. But still I wouldn't sleep until you came home,
late, school nights. One dim lamp in the living room, my dinner
simply thawed or boiled. And I left you, too, finally offered myself
up trembling, without pleasure, smarter and lovelier than him, but
never wanting to be a body.

Dear Manhood,

I watch the fat girls and the skinny girls, the fat women and the skinny women. I shrink and I grow in between. I trip down the steps, and hope no one has seen me. I spill wine on my work shirt, it sinks in the cuff, like blood. In my room, I have wooden cups full of little brushes, and boxes of paint for my face. I twist my feet into bony shoes every morning and I don't like to walk. At any moment, my body has six or more eyes staring at it, even if or especially when my body is naked and alone. I happen to have three sets of eyes, myself: these baby blues, my watching eyes, my hateful nictating membranes. If there is a lover with my body, or on my body, or in my body, he is always with, or on, or in, an idea of my body. My sweating cells, crying cells, bleeding cells, their ribosomes and golgi apparatus, my lobes, my lipids, my ducts and connective tissue, the fallopian and the limbic, the whole doomed apparatus is often abstracted into something to look at, or into a gesture that's as simple and disappointing as the hunger to degrade. There is nothing I can do about this abstraction. Did I ever know existence as something that is, and not as a thing to see? Sometimes I'd like to look like a million bucks, dear manhood, I really would, square and crisp, bank-vault cool.

Unplanned Conception

This story begins with suspecting Everything of not being O.K. I couldn't take my eyes off the fish's languid tail, the flicker like a slowed-down heartbeat. My lover, he threw his body down under a tiny desk for shelter, as if from something nuclear. Our trapped animal act. I bled for three days and watched movies in bed, he brought me ice cream. Sisters, I'm sorry for having wanted to eat anything at all. I threw up about a third of my soul and it looked and tasted exactly like bile. Yet several months later, as several months earlier, I was the one charged with taking in the other, between my breasts, as if he were my child.

In Vain

Belonging to a name was the beginning of disappointment. It was the beginning of vanity. This name, those words, assigned to me a body.

St. Audrey died of a tumour in her throat, which she considered to be just retribution, because in her youth she had for vain show adorned her neck with manifold splendid necklaces.

I will not write the words for fear that they will remain written. Making it true by saying it is so. I fear the vain words that reflect my name and my body as they manifest, continuously aging in the air of this world.

St. Audrey's lace (later shortened to "Tawdry lace") was a silk necktie much worn by women in the 16th century. It would naturally be largely offered for sale at her fair, and led to the production of cheap and showy forms for the "country wenches."

I would like to be offering something more beautiful than the words I choose, which must necessarily reflect my name and my body. More beautiful than I am.

"Tawdry" became shorthand for "cheap and pretentious finery."

I am most beautiful when I turn the page. My body is not reflected anywhere there, not on glass objects, electric screens, windows, metal surfaces, men's eyes, women's eyes.

Seventeen years after her death, St. Audrey's body was found to be incorrupt, proof of her steadfast virginity through two marriages.

The tumour on her neck, cut by her doctor, was found to be healed.
The linen cloths in which her body was wrapped were as fresh as the
day she had been buried.

Turning the page, I am nothing but the space between one word
and the other, the words choosing me.

Her
hair
grows
longer
by the
day
one
day
long
enough
to
bring
him
up
clutch
ing
clum
ps
in
hand
fuls
he
scales
the
wall
her
head
on
the
sill
the
hea
dac
hes
may
be
wo
rth
th
e
co
mp
a
n
y

Love Story

He sent several exclamation points my way. Something fell—no one uses those these days. I, on the other side, had had the courtesy to toss the clutter of the centuries, or give it to charity. Checkered dance floor, trellis, portico, all of the chambers, even the barely used valediction on an avenue (panting taxi, airport eyes). He made a proclamation and I swooned moments before the verb became extinct. Perhaps even now I can't comprehend the far-reaching implications of my previous statement. The only honest thing I can say: my digestive system plunged into a spin that could easily become a trope. No lovers have ever been legendary for being happy; happy shouldn't mean lucky. Listen, love, please listen. *No need to be novelesque. This is an invitation into the wonders of obscurity: protagonist of my gaze, amateur joy, not fit for publication.*

Notes

Part II of "Portrait of the President" uses elements of the life of Edwin Valero.

"Mongrel Tongue" references *Candide* by Voltaire.

"Let Your Hair Down" references information from *A Day in the Life of Ancient Rome* by Alberto Angela, translated by Gregory Conti, published by Europa Editions, 2009. The quote from the temple barber is from "Temple Hair Sale," BBC World Service, 24 June 2001, by Crispin Thorold, and the text on the origin of shaving women's heads is from "An Ugly Carnival," *The Guardian*, 4 June 2009, by Antony Beevor.

"In Vain" includes bits of the *Ecclesiasticall History* by the Venerable Bede, 731 AD and the Oxford English Dictionary entry on "tawdry."

Acknowledgements

I'm grateful to the editors of the following journals, which first published some of these poems, sometimes in a different form: *Barrelhouse, Barrow Street, Coconut, Denver Quarterly, The Homestead Review, The Inquisitive Eater, La Petite Zine, LIT, NOÖ Journal, Redivider, Sentence: A Journal of Prose Poetics,* and *Valley Voices.* Thanks, too, to the people behind the following presses, which shortlisted or otherwise supported the manuscript and gave it vital momentum: Barrow Street Press, Brooklyn Arts Press, Burnside Review Press, Cleveland State University Poetry Center, Gold Wake Press, and Tarpaulin Sky Press.

I would not be writing without the wisdom and encouragement of my teachers, in order of appearance: Monica Sparks, Bin Ramke, Laurie Sheck, Honor Moore, and Fanny Howe. A special thanks goes to another great teacher, David Lehman, for his unflagging kindness and moral support. I will be ever grateful to the poets and writers who have been gracious readers and kept my head above the water over the years: Melissa Broder, Wende Crow, Courtney Donner, Stacey Harwood-Lehman, Reb Livingston, Alexandra Mendez-Diez, Sharon Mesmer, Michael Quattrone, Amira Thoron, and Matthew Yeager. Laura Cronk actually dove into the water and pulled me out sometimes—thank you, sister. I also write in memory of the departed, Ruth Chaikin and Malinda Markham, two women whose generosity touched many lives, and who I won't forget.

Thank you to Sandra Doller, Daniel Borzutzky, the team at 1913 Press, and Olivia Croom for making this book possible. Thank you to Emmelien Brouwers for her compassion and insight. Thank you to my family for their love and support. And lastly, my love and thanks to Dan Méth for being a loyal consigliere, making me laugh at least once a day (including hard days), and for being a generous collaborator and artist ever-energized by creation.

Megin Jiménez was born in Mérida, Venezuela and grew up in Denver, USA. She studied at the University of Denver, Université Paris-Sorbonne, and The New School. She works as a translator and editor for international organizations and lives in the Netherlands.

Titles from 1913 Press

Pomme & Granite by Sarah Riggs (2015)

Untimely Death is Driven Out Beyond the Horizon
by Brenda Iijima (2015)

Full Moon Hawk Application by CA Conrad
(2014, Assless Chaps)

Big House/Disclosure by Mendi & Keith Obadike (2014)

Four Electric Ghosts by Mendi & Keith Obadike (2014)

O Human Microphone by Scott McFarland
(2014, selected by Rae Armantrout)

Kala Pani by Monica Mody (2013)

Bravura Cool by Jane Lewty (2012, selected by Fanny Howe)

The Transfer Tree by Karena Youtz (2012)

Conversities by Dan Beachy-Quick & Srikanth Reddy (2012)

Home/Birth: A Poemic by Arielle Greenberg & Rachel Zucker
(2011)

Wonderbender by Diane Wald (2011)

Ozalid by Biswamit Dwibedy (2010)

Sightings by Shin Yu Pai (2007)

Seismosis by John Keene & Christopher Stackhouse (2006)

Read 1-7, an annual anthology of inter-translation, Sarah Riggs
& Cole Swensen, eds.

1913 a journal of forms, Issues 1-6, Sandra Doller, ed.

Forthcoming

Conversations Over Stolen Food by Jon Cotner & Andy Fitch

Old Cat Lady: A Love Story in Possibilities by Lily Hoang

Strong Suits by Brad Flis

Epigraphe by Sophie Fetokaki

Disintegration Made Plain and Easy by Kiik Araki-Kawaguchi

1913 titles are distributed by Small Press Distribution:
www.spdbooks.org